We say we can no longer trust our public services, institutions or the people who run them. The professionals we have to rely on – politicians, doctors, scientists, businessmen and many others – are treated with suspicion. Their word is doubted, their motives questioned. Whether real or perceived, this crisis of trust has a debilitating impact on society and democracy. Can trust be restored by making people and institutions more accountable? Or do complex systems of accountability and control themselves damage trust? Onora O'Neill challenges current approaches, investigates sources of deception in our society and re-examines questions of press freedom. This year's Reith Lectures present a philosopher's view of trust and deception, and ask whether and how trust can be restored in a modern democracy.

ONORA O'NEILL is Principal of Newnham College, Cambridge. She has written widely on political philosophy and ethics, international justice, bioethics and the philosophy of Immanuel Kant. In 1999 she was made Baroness O'Neill of Bengarve and she sits in the House of Lords as a cross-bencher.

THE BBC REITH LECTURES 2002

A Question of Trust

ONORA O'NEILL

Principal
Newnham College, Cambridge

CAMBRIDGE
UNIVERSITY PRESS

PUBLISHED BY THE PRESS SYNDICATE OF THE UNIVERSITY OF CAMBRIDGE
The Pitt Building, Trumpington Street, Cambridge CB2 1RP, United Kingdom

CAMBRIDGE UNIVERSITY PRESS
The Edinburgh Building, Cambridge CB2 2RU, UK
40 West 20th Street, New York, NY 10011–4211, USA
477 Williamstown Road, Port Melbourne, VIC 3207, Australia
Ruiz de Alarcón 13, 28014 Madrid, Spain
Dock House, The Waterfront, Cape Town 8001, South Africa

http://www.cambridge.org

First published 2002

Printed in the United Kingdom at the University Press, Cambridge

Typeface Adobe Minion 11.5/17pt   *System* QuarkXPress® [PND]

A catalogue record for this book is available from the British Library

ISBN 0 521 82304 8 hardback
ISBN 0 521 52996 4 paperback

CONTENTS

PREFACE

Is it true that we have stopped trusting? Has untrustworthy action made trust too risky? Is trust obsolete?
In giving the Reith Lectures in the spring of 2002 I
began with these questions. It quickly became clear
that the evidence that we face a 'crisis of trust' is very
mixed. We often express suspicion, yet we constantly
place trust in others. Our attitudes and our action
diverge. Should we put our money where our mouths
are, and give up on trust? Or would giving up on trust
just be a matter of placing more trust in abstract
systems of control and audit?

Trusting is not a matter of blind deference, but of
placing – or refusing – trust with good judgement. So
we need social and political institutions that allow us
to judge where to place our trust. Yet some fashionable ways of trying to make institutions and professionals trustworthy undermine our abilities to place

and refuse trust with discrimination. We proclaim human rights with enthusiasm, but don't ask whether the rights are compatible with one another, or whether the corresponding duties are feasible. We set detailed performance targets for public bodies, but are complacent about the perverse incentives they create. We try to micro-manage complex institutions from the centre, and wonder why we get over-complex and inadequate rather than good and effective governance. We try to judge quality by performance indicators rather than by seeking informed and independent evaluation. We aspire to complete transparency in public life, but neglect the more fundamental goal of limiting deception. We endorse a version of press freedom that is not supported by the reasons why we need a free press.

The lectures were fun to give. I would like to thank the BBC for inviting me, and Sue Lawley, Gwynneth Williams and Charlie Sigler, as well as Sue Collins, for helping me in many ways.

Onora O'Neill, Newnham College, Cambridge

April 2002

I

Spreading suspicion

1 'Without trust we cannot stand'

Confucius told his disciple Tzu-kung that three things are needed for government: weapons, food and trust.[1] If a ruler can't hold on to all three, he should give up the weapons first and the food next. Trust should be guarded to the end: without trust we cannot stand. Confucius' thought still convinces. Weapons did not help the Taliban when their foot soldiers lost trust and deserted. Food shortages need not topple governments when they and their rationing systems are trusted, as we know from the Second World War.

It isn't only rulers and governments who prize and need trust. Each of us and every profession and every

[1] Arthur Waley, *The Analects of Confucius* (London: George Allen and Unwin, 1938), xii, 7, p. 164.

institution needs trust. We need it because we have to be able to rely on others acting as they say that they will, and because we need others to accept that we will act as we say we will. The sociologist Niklas Luhmann was right that 'A complete absence of trust would prevent [one] even getting up in the morning.'[2]

2 The crisis of trust

We may need trust, but trusting often seems hard and risky. Every day we read of untrustworthy action by politicians and officials, by hospitals and exam boards, by companies and schools. We supposedly face a deepening crisis of trust. Every day we also read of aspirations and attempts to make business and professionals, public servants and politicians more accountable in more ways to more stakeholders. But can a revolution in accountability remedy our 'crisis of trust'?

In these five chapters I shall discuss both the

2 Niklas Luhmann, *Trust* (Chichester: John Wiley & Sons, 1979), p. 4.

supposed crisis and its supposed remedies. I do so as an outsider. The experts and exponents of the crisis of trust are mainly sociologists and journalists: they've tried to find out whom we do and don't trust, in particular whom we *say* we do and don't trust. They have produced lots of dispiriting evidence. Remedies are proposed on all sides: politicians and campaigning groups, academics and journalists advocate greater respect for human rights, higher standards of accountability and greater transparency. If these are remedies for our 'crisis of trust', we should surely be seeing results by now. On the contrary, the accusations mount.

I shall look at trust from a more philosophical but also (I hope) more practical standpoint: these (I believe) go together quite naturally. What does it take for us to place trust in others? What evidence do we need to place it well? Are human rights and democracy the basis for a society in which trust can be placed, or does trust need other conditions? Does the revolution in accountability support or undermine trust?

The common ground from which I begin is that we

cannot have guarantees that everybody will keep trust. Elaborate measures to ensure that people keep agreements and do not betray trust must, in the end, be backed by – trust. At some point we just have to trust. There is no *complete* answer to the old question: 'who will guard the guardians?' On the contrary, trust is needed precisely because all guarantees are incomplete. Guarantees are useless unless they lead to a trusted source, and a regress of guarantees is no better for being longer unless it ends in a trusted source. So trust cannot presuppose or require a watertight guarantee of others' performance, and cannot rationally be withheld just because we lack guarantees. Where we have guarantees or proofs, placing trust is redundant. We don't need to take it on trust that $5 \times 11 = 55$, or that we are alive, or that each of us was born of a human mother or that the sun rose this morning.

Since trust has to be placed without guarantees, it is inevitably sometimes misplaced: others let us down and we let others down. When this happens, trust and relationships based on trust are both damaged. Trust, it is constantly observed, is hard earned and easily dissipated. It is valuable social capital and not to be squandered.

If there are no guarantees to be had, we need to place trust with care. This can be hard. The little shepherd boy who shouted 'Wolf! Wolf!' eventually lost his sheep, but not before his false alarms had deceived others time and again. Deception and betrayal often work. Traitors and terrorists, embezzlers and con artists, forgers and plagiarists, false promisers and free riders cultivate then breach others' trust. They often get away with it. Breach of trust has been around since the Garden of Eden – although it did not quite work out there. Now it is more varied and ingenious, and often successful.

Although we cannot curse those who breach trust, let alone expel them from paradise, we take elaborate steps to deter and prevent deception and fraud: we set and enforce high standards. Human rights requirements are imposed on the law, on institutions, on all of us. Contracts clarify and formalise agreements and undertakings with ever-greater precision. Professional codes define professional responsibilities with ever-greater precision.

Huge efforts also go into ensuring trustworthy performance. Auditors scrutinise accounts (but are they trustworthy?). Examiners control and mark examinees (but are they trustworthy?). The police investigate crimes (but are they trustworthy?). Increasingly sophisticated technologies are deployed to prevent and detect breaches of trust, ranging from locks and safes, passwords and identity cards, to CCTV cameras and elaborate encryption. The efforts to prevent abuse of trust are gigantic, relentless and expensive; their results are always less than perfect.

Have these countermeasures begun to restore trust, or to reduce suspicion? Sociologists and journalists report few signs. They claim that we are in the grip of a deepening crisis of public trust that is directed even at our most familiar institutions and office-holders. Mistrust, it seems, is now directed not just at those clearly in breach of law and accepted standards, not just at crooks and wide boys. Mistrust and suspicion have spread across all areas of life, and supposedly with good reason. Citizens, it is said, no longer trust governments, or politicians, or ministers, the police, or the courts, or the prison service.

Consumers, it is said, no longer trust business, and especially big business, or their products. *None of us,* it is said, trusts banks, or insurers – or pension providers. Patients, it is said, no longer trust doctors (think of Dr Shipman!), and in particular no longer trust hospitals or hospital consultants. 'Loss of trust' has become a cliché of our times.

How good is the evidence for this crisis of trust? A lot of the most systematic evidence for the UK can be found in public opinion polls and analogous academic surveys. The pollsters ask carefully controlled cross-sections of the public whether they trust certain professions or office-holders. The questions aren't easy to answer. Most of us would want to say that we trust *some* but not *other* professionals, *some* but not *other* office-holders, in *some* matters but not in *others.* I might trust a schoolteacher to teach my child arithmetic but not citizenship. I might trust my GP to diagnose and prescribe for a sore throat, but not for a heart attack. I might trust my bank with my current account, but not with my life savings. In answering the pollsters we suppress the complexity of our real judgements, smooth out distinctions we draw between different individuals and institutions, and average our judgements about their trustworthiness in different activities.

We depend on journalists for our knowledge of the results of these polls and the levels of reported public trust. There is some irony in this, since these polls repeatedly show that no profession is less trusted in the UK than journalism. Journalists – at least newspaper journalists – are typically less trusted than politicians and ministers, much less trusted than scientists and civil servants, and dramatically less trusted than judges, or ministers of religion or doctors. Of course, the public also draws distinctions within these categories. Nurses and GPs are more trusted than hospital consultants; university scientists are more trusted than industry scientists; television news presenters are more trusted than newspaper journalists. Often newspaper reports of public opinion highlight the most dramatic statistic, typically the one that suggests the most extreme mistrust. They seldom comment on the ambiguities of the questions or the categories, or linger on cases where trust is average or high.

3 Active trust

The polls supposedly show that in the UK public trust in office-holders and professionals of many sorts is low and declining. They certainly reveal a mood of suspicion. But do they show anything more? Are the opinions we divulge to pollsters backed up by the ways in which we *actively* place our trust in others, and specifically by the ways that we place it, or refuse to place it, in public servants, professionals and institutions?

Much of the evidence of the way we actively place our trust seems to me to point in quite different directions. We constantly place trust in others, in members of professions and in institutions. Nearly all of us drink water provided by water companies and eat food sold in supermarkets and produced by ordinary farming practices. Nearly all of us use the roads (and, even more rationally, the trains!). Nearly all of us listen to the news and buy newspapers. Even if we have some misgivings, we go on placing trust in medicines produced by the pharmaceutical industry, in operations performed in NHS hospitals, in the delivery of letters by the Post Office, and in roads shared with many notably imperfect drivers. We constantly place active trust in many others.

Does action speak louder than words? Are the ways we actually place our trust a more accurate gauge of trust than our comments to pollsters? If we were really as mistrusting as some of us tell the pollsters, would we behave like this? We might do so if we had no options. Perhaps the fact of the matter is that we simply have to *rely* on institutions and persons although we *don't really trust them*. In many of these examples, it may seem, we have little choice. How can we avoid tap water, even if we mistrust the water companies, since it is the only ready source of supply? How can we avoid conventional medicines, even if we mistrust the pharmaceutical industry, since there are no effective and affordable alternatives? How can we avoid the news as (mis)represented, if we have no other sources?

But are these thoughts really convincing? Those who *seriously* mistrust producers and suppliers of consumer goods *can* and *do* refuse to rely on them. Those who *really* mistrust the tap water drink bottled water, or boil it, or use water purification tablets: where water supplies are *seriously* questionable, people do so. Those who *really* mistrust the pharmaceutical industry and its products can refuse them and choose to rely on alternative, more natural, remedies. Those who *really* mistrust the newspapers can stop buying them – although this may not put them wholly beyond the reach of the opinions, 'stories' and attitudes that journalists purvey. Those who *really* mistrust the standards of food safety of conventional agriculture, food processing, shops and restaurants can eat organically grown food: it may cost more, but is less expensive than convenience foods and eating out. Where people have options we can tell whether they *really* mistrust by seeing whether they put their money where they put their mouths. The evidence suggests that we still constantly place trust in many of the institutions and professions we profess not to trust.

Evidence for trust or mistrust is less clear when opting out is hard or impossible. There is no way of opting out of public goods – or public harms. We have to breathe the ambient air we share – even if we don't trust standards for monitoring air pollution. We can't help relying on the police to protect us, since they have a monopoly of law enforcement – even if we are suspicious of them. We cannot opt out of government, or the legal system or the currency, even if we have misgivings. What should we think when people say they do not trust the providers and suppliers of public goods and services on which they have to rely? It seems to me that where people have no choice, their action provides *poor* evidence that they trust – or that they mistrust.

Where we have no choice, the only evidence of mistrust is what people say. But we know from cases where they have choice that this can be unreliable evidence. If what we say is unreliable evidence when we have choices, why should we think it reliable evidence when we have no choices? Expressions of mistrust that are divorced from action come cheap: we can assert and rescind, flaunt or change, defend or drop attitudes and expressions of mistrust without changing the way we live. This may show something about attitudes of suspicion, but little or nothing about where we place trust.

4 Trust and risk

So is there other evidence for a crisis of trust? Do we trust less today, or are we just more inclined to spread suspicion? Are current levels of mistrust greater than those of the past? Adequate evidence for a new crisis of trust must do more than point to *some* untrustworthy doctors and scientists, *some* untrustworthy companies and politicians, *some* untrustworthy fraudsters and colleagues. There have always been breaches of trust, and examples alone can't show we are living amid a new or deeper crisis of trust.

Some sociologists have suggested that the crisis of trust is real and new because we now live in a *risk society*. We live among highly complex institutions and practices whose effects we cannot control or understand, and supposedly see ourselves as subject to hidden and incomprehensible sources of risk. *Individuals* can do little or nothing to avert environmental risks, or nuclear accidents or terrorist attacks.

This is true, but not new. The harms and hazards modern societies impose differ from those in traditional societies. But there is nothing new about inability to reduce risk, about ignorance of its sources, or about not being able to opt out. Those who saw their children die of tuberculosis in the nineteenth century, those who could do nothing to avert swarming locusts or galloping infectious disease, and those who struggled with sporadic food shortage and fuel poverty through history might be astonished to discover that anyone thinks that ours rather than theirs is a risk society. So might those in the developing world who live with chronic food scarcity or drought, endemic corruption or lack of security. If the developed world is the paradigm of a 'risk society', risk societies must be characterised simply by their *perceptions of* and *attitudes to* risk, and not by the seriousness of the hazards to which people are exposed, or the likelihood that those hazards will harm them.

So is the current supposed crisis of trust just a public mood or attitude of suspicion, rather than a proper and justified response to growing untrustworthiness? Those who speak and write of a 'crisis of trust' generally assume that *we* have justifiably stopped trusting because *they* are less trustworthy. I hope I have shown that the evidence for this claim is pretty mixed. Of course, today as always, there are plenty of examples of untrustworthy individuals, officials, professionals and politicians. But examples do not show that there is *on balance* more untrustworthy behaviour today than there was in the past. Nothing follows from *examples* of sporadic untrustworthiness, however flamboyant, except the sober truth that today – as always – not everybody is wholly trustworthy and trust must be placed with care. Without the full range of evidence – including full evidence of trustworthy action – we cannot draw sound conclusions about a new or deepening crisis of trust. Unless we take account of the good news of trustworthiness as well as the bad news of untrustworthiness, we won't know whether we have a crisis of trust or only a culture of suspicion. In my view it isn't surprising that if we persist in viewing good news as no news at all, we end up viewing no news at all as good news. The crisis of trust may be an article of faith: but where is our evidence for it?

5 Some new suspicions

We may not have evidence for a crisis of trust; but we have massive evidence of a culture of suspicion. Let me briefly join that culture of suspicion, and finish by voicing some suspicions of my own that I shall trace in the next four chapters. My first suspicion falls on one of our most sacred cows: the human rights movement. We fantasise irresponsibly that we can promulgate rights without thinking carefully about the counterpart obligations, and without checking whether the rights we favour are consistent, let alone set feasible demands on those who have to secure them for others. My suspicions fall secondly on our new conceptions of accountability, which superimpose managerial targets on bureaucratic process, burdening and even paralysing those who have to comply. My suspicions fall thirdly on the new ideal of the information age: transparency, which has marginalised the more basic obligation not to deceive. My suspicion falls finally on our public culture, which is so often credulous about its own standards of communication and suspicious of everyone else's. We need *genuine* rights, *genuine* accountability, *genuine* efforts to reduce deception, and *genuine* communication. We are pursuing distorted versions of each of them.

Perhaps claims about a crisis of trust are mainly evidence of an unrealistic hankering for a world in which safety and compliance are total, and breaches of trust are totally eliminated. Perhaps the culture of accountability that we are relentlessly building for ourselves actually damages trust rather than supporting it. Plants don't flourish when we pull them up too often to check how their roots are growing: political, institutional and professional life too may not flourish if we constantly uproot it to demonstrate that everything is transparent and trustworthy.

2

Trust and terror

1 Daily trust

We all first learn to trust and what it takes to be trust-worthy as small children, from family, friends and neighbours. I first learned about trust in the Braid Valley near Belfast, where I was born and spent large parts of my childhood in my grandparents' home. Despite the political tensions that all families in Northern Ireland know, trust was strong: doors were not locked and questions were answered honestly.

For all of us trust is the most everyday thing. Every day and in hundreds of ways we trust others to do what they say, to play by the rules and to behave reasonably. We trust other drivers to steer safely; we trust postal staff to deliver letters efficiently – more or less; we trust teachers to prepare our children for exams; we trust colleagues to do what they say; we even trust strangers to tell us the way.

In placing trust we don't simply assume that others are reliable and predictable, as we assume that the sun rises reliably, and the milk goes off predictably. When we trust, we know – at least once we are no longer children – that we could be disappointed. Sometimes we place trust despite past disappointment, or without much evidence of reliability. To withdraw trust after a single lapse, as if we were rejecting a scientific theory in the face of decisive contrary evidence, would often be suspicious, even paranoid. All trust risks disappointment. The risk of disappointment, even of betrayal, cannot be written out of our lives. As Samuel Johnson put it 'it is happier to be sometimes cheated than not to trust'.[1] Trust is needed not because everything is wholly predictable, let alone wholly guaranteed, but on the contrary because life has to be led without guarantees.

1   Samuel Johnson, *The Rambler*, no. 79, vol. ii, ed. W. J. Bate and Albrecht B. Strauss (New Haven: Yale University Press, 1969).

2 Trust and fear

Trust often invites reciprocal trust: there are virtuous spirals. Equally trust can open the door to betrayal, and betrayal to mistrust: there are vicious spirals. Here I want to say something about the most extreme situations when trust starts spiralling downwards, and we may lose it altogether.

In dangerous times placing trust is risky. Holding fire may allow an enemy to fire first and fatally; refusal to denounce may allow another terrified person to get a denunciation in first. Prisoners' dilemmas are not just abstract theory – they really happen. And this last year terrorism has been more than ever in our minds. Terrorism undermines the conditions of trust less because it inflicts violence – the violence may be sporadic – than because it spreads fear. As the etymology of the word tells us, terrorists aim at terror, at fear, at intimidation. Fear and intimidation corrode and undermine our ability to place trust, declining trust in turn fuels pre-emptive action and hostilities, and makes it harder to trust.

Events in New York illustrate this all too well. The US lives with a great deal of sporadic violence: crime and the gun culture flourish. This violence creates a good deal of fear – mainly private fear, allayed (in part) by ingenious private security; but it does not wholly undermine the possibility of trust in others and in public institutions The collapse of those gleaming towers led to wider fears that no private security arrangements could reduce. It made the daily placing of trust in others and in the normal functioning of public institutions harder. Fear intruded into the seemingly well-protected spaces of the office and the airport, the Pentagon and the Stock Exchange. The spread of fear caused by the atrocities, and by the anthrax mailings, was the more palpable because nobody spelt out how further terrorism could be averted.

This was not coercive terror, of the sort practised by the Mafia and reasonably well known in Belfast and many other places; it was not 'an offer you cannot refuse'; it was abrupt and unpredictable rather than sticking to a sickeningly familiar pattern. There was no statement of terms to be met; nobody claimed so-called 'credit'. There was only the obscurity and silence of pure terror. Subsequent events have made the identities and aims of the perpetrators of 11th September a bit less obscure; those behind the anthrax mailings remain wholly obscure.

3 Trust, rights and democracy

Where danger and terror undermine trust, nothing is more urgent than restoring conditions for trust. But how is this to be done? One standard contemporary answer is that the political conditions for placing trust must be achieved, and that these include human rights and democracy. Human rights and democracy have both been central to efforts to construct a 'peace process' in Northern Ireland, and in other parts of the world. I believe that human rights and democracy are not the basis of trust: on the contrary, trust is basic for human rights and democracy.

Human rights are more often gestured at than they are seriously argued for. The list of rights proclaimed in the *Universal Declaration of Human Rights* of 1948 is often seen as canonical. But the list is untidy and unargued. It includes some rights of high importance that may be universal rights. It also includes culturally narrow rights, such as the 'right to holidays with pay': this supposed right was an aspiration of the labour movement in the developed world in the mid twentieth century; it has little relevance for the billions of human beings who are not employees.

The *Declaration* defines rights poorly, and says almost nothing about the corresponding duties. No inspection of the *Universal Declaration*, or of later UN or European documents, shows *who* is required to do *what* for *whom*, or *why* they are required to do it. The underlying difficulty of any declaration of rights is that it assumes a *passive* view of human life and of citizenship. Rights answer the questions 'What are my entitlements?' or 'What should I get?' They don't answer the active citizen's question 'What should I do?'

Yet no claim to rights has the faintest chance of making a real difference without clear answers to the question 'What should I do?' A supposed right to free speech is mere rhetoric unless others – *all* competent others – have duties to respect free speech. A supposed right to a fair trial is mere rhetoric unless others – *all* relevant others – have duties to ensure such trials: unless judges have duties to give fair decisions, unless police and witnesses have duties to testify, and to testify honestly, and so on for all involved in a legal process. Duties are the business end of justice: they formulate the requirements towards which declarations of rights gesture; they speak to all of us whose action is vital for real, respected rights.

If duties are the business end of ethical and political requirements, why do we lavish so much more attention on rights? And why are we so often silent or slipshod in talking and thinking about duties? Perhaps it is partly because it is more fun to think about all the things that others should do for us, than it is to think about what we should do for them.

But there may be deeper, more political reasons. Declarations of rights ostensibly offer something to everybody, without coming clean about the costs and demands of respecting the rights they proclaim. Governments have generally been willing to sign up to declarations of rights, indeed to ratify them, but less keen to meet the counterpart duties. Individuals have often been willing, even eager, to claim rights, but less willing to meet their duties to respect others' rights. In thinking about rights we readily see ourselves on the receiving end – and it is always someone else's round.

The *Universal Declaration* takes a simple and unsatisfactory view of the duties needed to secure rights: it assigns them to *states*. It conveniently ignores the reality that some states are not committed to rights and that others are too weak to secure them.

Where states or parts of states are weak or failing, it is idle to object when they do not secure full rights for all: they can't. Rights are not taken seriously unless the duties that underpin them are also taken seriously; those duties are not taken seriously unless there are effective and committed people and institutions that can do what they require. How can there be rights to fair trials when terrorists cannot be prosecuted for their crimes because witnesses know that it is beyond the power of the police to protect them if they testify? How can rights to freedom of assembly be secure in the face of intimidation? How can basic civic rights be secured in a country of well-armed clans like Afghanistan? How can fair trials proceed where judges are bribed or menaced, or even assassinated?

Without competent and committed persons and institutions, duties are not met; where they are not met, rights are not respected; and where rights are not respected, democracy is unachievable. Democracy can show us what is politically legitimate; it can't show us what is ethically justified. On the contrary democracy *presupposes* rights, and rights presuppose duties. There can be no full democracy where rights and duties are violated, where voters are intimidated, where ballot boxes are stuffed or where political parties working within the constitution are banned.

4 Which duties?

If duties (or *obligations*) *are prior to rights*[2] we need to reorient our political thinking. This thought is quite

---

2 Simone Weil, *The Need for Roots: a Prelude to a Declaration of Duties towards Mankind*, trans. A. F. Wills (London: Routledge and Kegan Paul, 1952).

different from the familiar platitude that we all have responsibilities as well as rights. The platitude is false. Babies and the severely retarded have rights but no responsibilities. But if any of us is to have any rights, others must have counterpart duties. The thought that nobody has rights unless others have duties is a precise logical claim. So in thinking about ethics and politics we would do better to begin by thinking about *what* ought to be done and *who* ought to do it, rather than about what we ought to get. Passive citizens, who wait for others to accord their rights and mistakenly suppose that states alone can secure them, are doomed to disappointment. Active citizens who meet their duties thereby secure one another's rights.

Active citizens take a serious view of their duties. This cannot be done by looking up some *Declaration of Human Duties* – although this unfashionable literary genre at least addresses the proper question. How then can we know which duties, and in particular which political duties, are fundamental? One way of thinking about this, which I find more convincing than any alternative, derives from the work of

Immanuel Kant, the great eighteenth-century philosopher who lived at the far end of Europe, in remote East Prussia on the boundaries of Russia. He sees duty as the basis of rights and of justice and his famous arguments for cosmopolitan justice have made him one of the most significant political thinkers in our globalising age – in spite of his demanding thought and sometimes tortured prose.

So let me begin with the Kantian thought that we are all moral equals. Nowadays this thought is usually followed up with the claim that we all have equal rights. But for Kant the deeper implication is that we all have equal duties. No competent person, and none of the institutions that human beings construct, is exempt from fundamental duties. The basic principles of justice – like all ethical principles – are *principles for all*. We should not therefore act on principles that are unfit to be principles for all.

This is a tough requirement. It is always easy to think that one's own case or cause is exceptional. Violence and terror, coercion and murder, intimidation and mutilation have victims: perpetrators know and intend to ensure that those victims are unable to do what they themselves do. They know *from the start* that their ways of acting are not open to their victims, hence not open to all others. Equally, deception and fraud, extortion and manipulation, have victims: perpetrators know and intend to ensure that those victims are unable to do what they themselves do. They know *from the start* that their ways of acting are not open to their victims, and hence not open to all others. Anybody who aims to act only on principles that others too can adopt must reject these and all other ways of victimising.

These robust and demanding conclusions identify basic duties that must be met if we are to live in a world in which trust can be placed, in which institutions that secure human rights can be built, and in which democracy may be possible. Where violence and coercion, deception and intimidation are common, it is because some people act on principles that cannot be principles for all: they breach and neglect fundamental duties and in doing so violate others' rights, and undermine both democracy and the placing of trust.

5 Trust during dark times

These arguments show that we have duties that provide a basis for rights and democracy. But they don't show what citizens should do when others flout their duties. Why should anyone place trust, fulfil fundamental duties or respect others' rights if they face intimidation and violence, extortion and deception, and at the limit terror? Won't those who place trust or meet duties in these conditions face danger and become victims?

If we think rights are the *precondition* of social and political trust, there is nothing *we* can do until *other* people start respecting *our* rights – and nothing *they* can do until *we* start respecting *their* rights. If we persist in taking a passive view of human beings, seeing them primarily as holders of rights, and forgetting that those rights are the flip side of others' duties, restoring trust may seem a hopeless task. But if we remember that human beings must act before *anyone* can have rights there is a different way of looking at matters. Some duties that support trust can be met even in the darkest times.

As we read the inspiring literatures on confronting terror and oppression in many parts of the world in recent decades, we can see how small moves can begin large changes. Let me give you an example not from South Africa, or Chile or Northern Ireland, but from former Czechoslovakia. In his wonderful essay 'Power of the Powerless' President Václav Havel describes a way in which it was possible to refuse complicity with injustice in the dark days before the Velvet Revolution. The Communist Party of the People's Republic of Czechoslovakia used to send bulletins with Party slogans and messages to be displayed in all shops. These mind-numbingly boring Party slogans were so familiar that they became invisible: yet displaying them represented support for the regime and its oppressions, a small connivance, a small lie. Refusal to display those slogans, to endorse that view of the world, was a small act of truth and courage, and ultimately of power, that was open to the powerless. From small refusals larger and bolder action followed.

Lying, complicity and refusal to testify honestly are common in the face of fear and terror; but they can be built down rather than reinforced. This can be done by rejecting the politically correct vocabulary in which crimes are renamed, and perpetrators accorded respectability; by refusing to lie and by telling more of the truth; by refusing to endorse slogans and half-truths. Trust is destroyed by deception: destroying deception builds trust – and thereby a basis for rights and democracy.

Of course, there are conditions so dire that even minor defiance is risky: in Stalin's Soviet Union and in Taliban Afghanistan trivial non-conformity could have exorbitant costs; only underground resistance was possible. But beyond the extremes there are possibilities. Refusing complicity does not damage but creates a climate for trust. We can stop using euphemisms to placate those who threaten or do injustice; we can refuse to dignify community intimidators by speaking of them as community leaders; we can accord genuine community leaders the honour they deserve. We can stop using vocabularies of community protection and freedom fighting to dignify crimes. We can stop calling for reduced police powers while demanding stronger police protection.

We can set aside the passive outlook, which fantasises that blaming and accusing others contributes to justice.

In offering these examples I do not mean to suggest that we need heroes rather than reform. On the contrary, active citizens improve institutions as they improve the conditions of trust. Increasing performance of duties builds a foundation for human rights and for democracy, and may start a virtuous spiral of trust. In the past fifty years we have too often modelled justice in terms of human rights, thoughtlessly assuming that states can shoulder the entire task of securing rights and blaming them when they fail. We have closed our eyes to the inadequacy of state power in many parts of the world and to its limits wherever people take a merely passive view of citizenship.

Terror is the ultimate denial and destroyer of trust. Terrorists violate the spectrum of human duties and thereby the spectrum of human rights. Typically they do violence and coerce, they deceive and intimidate. In the wake of terror, trust spirals downwards. Its restoration is the hardest of political and civic tasks: it is not a task that states can handle alone. The passive culture of human rights suggests that we can sit back and wait for others to deliver our entitlements. If we really want human rights we have to act – and to meet our duties to one another.

3

Called to account

1 Is trust failing?

Like many of us, I live and work among professionals and public servants. And those whom I know seek to serve the public conscientiously – and mostly to pretty good effect. Addenbrooke's, for example, is an outstanding hospital; the University of Cambridge and many surrounding research institutions do distinguished work; Cambridgeshire schools, social services and police have good reputations. Yet during the last fifteen years we have all found our reputations and performance doubted, as have millions of other public sector workers and professionals. We increasingly hear that we are no longer trusted.

A standard account of the supposed 'crisis of public trust' is that the public rightly no longer trusts professionals and public servants because they are less trustworthy. But is this true? A look at past news reports would show that there has always been some failure and some abuse of trust; other cases may never have seen the light of day. Since we never know how much untrustworthy action is undetected, we can hardly generalise.

Growing mistrust would be a reasonable response to growing untrustworthiness; but the evidence that people or institutions are less trustworthy is elusive.

In fact I think there isn't even very good evidence that we trust less. There *is* good evidence that we *say* we trust less: we tell the pollsters, they tell the media, and the news that we say we do not trust is then put into circulation. But saying repeatedly that we don't trust no more shows that we trust less, than an echo shows the truth of the echoed words; still less does it show that others are less trustworthy.

Could our actions provide better evidence than our words and show that we do indeed trust less than we used to? Curiously I think that our action often provides evidence that we still trust. We may *say* we don't trust hospital consultants, and yet apparently we want operations – and we are pretty cross if they get delayed. We may *say* that we don't trust the police, but then we call them when trouble threatens. We may *say* that we don't trust scientists and engineers, but then we rely on hi-tech clinical tests and medical devices. The supposed 'crisis of trust' may be more a matter of what we tell inquisitive pollsters than of any active refusal of trust, let alone of conclusive evidence of reduced trustworthiness. The supposed 'crisis of trust' is, I think, first and foremost a culture of suspicion.

2 More perfect accountability?

The diagnosis of a crisis of trust may be obscure: we are not sure whether there is a crisis of trust. But we are all agreed about the remedy. It lies in prevention and sanctions. Government, institutions and professionals should be made more accountable. And in the last two decades, the quest for greater accountability has penetrated all our lives, like great draughts of Heineken, reaching parts that supposedly less developed forms of accountability did not reach.

For those of us in the public sector the new

accountability takes the form of detailed control. An unending stream of new legislation and regulation, memoranda and instructions, guidance and advice floods into public sector institutions. For example, a look into the vast database of documents on the Department of Health website arouses a mixture of despair and disbelief. Central planning may have failed in the former Soviet Union but it is alive and well in Britain today. The new accountability culture aims at ever more perfect administrative control of institutional and professional life.

The new legislation, regulation and controls are more than fine rhetoric. They require detailed conformity to procedures and protocols, detailed record-keeping and provision of information in specified formats *and* success in reaching targets. Detailed instructions regulate and prescribe the work and performance of health trusts and schools, of universities and research councils, of the police force and of social workers. And beyond the public sector, increasingly detailed legislative and regulatory requirements also bear on companies and the voluntary sector, on self-employed professionals and tradesmen. All institutions face new standards of recommended accounting practice, more detailed health and safety requirements, increasingly complex employment and pensions legislation, more exacting provisions for ensuring non-discrimination and, of course, proliferating complaint procedures.

The new accountability has quite sharp teeth. Performance is monitored and subjected to quality control and quality assurance. The idea of *audit* has been exported from its original financial context to cover ever more detailed scrutiny of non-financial processes and systems. Performance indicators are used to measure adequate and inadequate performance with supposed precision. This *audit explosion*, as Michael Power has so aptly called it, has often displaced or marginalised older systems of accountability.[1] In the universities, external examiners lost influence as centrally planned teaching quality assessment was imposed; in the health services, professional judgement is constrained in many ways; in schools, curriculum and assessment of pupils are controlled

1 Michael Power, *The Audit Society: Rituals of Verification* (Oxford: Oxford University Press, 1997).

in pretty minute detail. Schools, hospitals and universities are then all judged and funded by their rankings in league tables of performance indicators.

Managerial accountability for achieving targets is also imposed on institutions although they are given little institutional freedom. Hospital Trusts may be self-governing, but they do not choose which patients to admit or what standards of care to provide. School governors and head teachers have few discretionary powers: they may not select their pupils or expel those whose exam performance will damage their rankings. Universities are supposedly still autonomous, but they have little choice but to cut or close departments with lower research ratings who lose their funding. We are supposedly on the high road towards ever more perfect accountability. Well, I wonder.

3 Accountability and mistrust

Have these instruments for control, regulation, monitoring and enforcement worked? Their effects are certainly pretty evident in the daily lives of conscientious professionals and administrators. Professionals have to work to ever more exacting – if changing – standards of good practice and due process, to meet relentless demands to record and report, and they are subject to regular ranking and restructuring. I think that many public sector professionals find that the new demands damage their real work. Teachers aim to teach their pupils; nurses to care for their patients; university lecturers to do research and to teach; police officers to deter and apprehend those whose activities harm the community; social workers to help those whose lives are for various reasons unmanageable or very difficult. Each profession has its proper aim, and this aim is not reducible to meeting set targets following prescribed procedures and requirements.

If the new methods and requirements supported and didn't obstruct the real purposes of each of these professions and institutions, the accountability revolution might achieve its aims. Unfortunately I think it often obstructs the proper aims of professional practice. Police procedures for preparing cases are so demanding that fewer cases can be prepared, and

fewer criminals brought to court. Doctors speak of
the inroads that required record-keeping makes into
the time that they can spend finding out what is
wrong with their patients and listening to their
patients. Even children are not exempt from the new
accountability: exams are more frequent and time for
learning shrinks. In many parts of the public sector,
complaint procedures are so burdensome that avoid-
ing complaints, including ill-founded complaints,
becomes a central institutional goal in its own right.
We are heading towards defensive medicine, defensive teaching and defensive policing.

The new accountability is widely experienced not
just as *changing* but (I think) as *distorting the proper
aims of professional practice* and indeed as damaging
professional pride and integrity. Much professional
practice used to centre on interaction with those
whom professionals serve: patients and pupils,
students and families in need. Now there is less time
to do this because everyone has to record the details
of what they do and compile the evidence to protect
themselves against the possibility not only of plausi-
ble, but of far-fetched complaints. We are now told

that officers on the beat will have to record what they take to be the ethnic background of anyone whom they stop and search. I think that the mistaken ethnic classifications will offer a very rich source of future complaints. Professionals and public servants understandably end up responding to requirements and targets and not only to those whom they are supposed to serve.

Well, are these thoughts just accomplished professional whingeing? Those who are bent on ever-improving standards of performance and accountability generally think so. Professions and public service, they remind us, serve the public. If life is less cosy, if familiar shortcuts are abolished, if everybody is made more accountable, if old boy networks are undermined, if poor performance is detected and penalised, isn't this exactly what we want a revolution in accountability to achieve? If the revolution of accountability has yet to deliver the goods, should we not prescribe more of the same?

But I'd like to suggest that the revolution in accountability be judged by the standards that it proposes. If it is working we might expect to see indications –

performance indicators! – that public trust is reviving. But we don't. In the very years in which the accountability revolution has made striking advances, in which increased demands for control and performance, scrutiny and audit have been imposed, and in which the performance of professionals and institutions has been more and more controlled, we find in fact growing reports of mistrust. In my view these expressions of mistrust suggest that just possibly we are imposing the wrong sorts of accountability. The new systems of control may have aims and effects that are quite distinct from the higher standards of performance, monitoring and accountability that are their ostensible, publicly celebrated aims. We can see this by asking *to whom* the new audit culture makes professionals and institutions accountable, and *for what* it makes them accountable.

In theory the new culture of accountability and audit makes professionals and institutions more accountable *to the public.* This is supposedly done by publishing targets and levels of attainment in league tables, and by establishing complaint procedures by which members of the public can seek redress for any professional or institutional failures. But underlying this ostensible aim of accountability *to the public* the real requirements are for accountability *to regulators, to departments of government, to funders, to legal standards.* The new forms of accountability impose forms of *central control* – quite often indeed a *range of different and mutually inconsistent* forms of central control.

Some of the new modes of public accountability are in fact internally incoherent. Some of them set targets that cannot be combined without fudging: for example, universities are soon to be told to admit 50 per cent of the age group, but also to maintain current standards. Others are incoherent because they require that targets be achieved by following processes that do not dovetail with targets and can't be made to dovetail with those targets. Again, universities are to treat each applicant fairly on the basis of ability and promise – but they are supposed also to admit a socially more representative intake. There's no guarantee that the process meets the target. Hospitals are to treat each patient on a basis of need and prioritise emergencies, but they are going to be criticised if they postpone non-urgent operations. That might be legitimate grounds for criticism if they could build in spare capacity and do the non-urgent as well as the urgent operations. But the NHS has been made tightly efficient in its use of resources, so it cannot build in spare capacity on the necessary scale. Schools are to prevent classroom disruption – but they are not to exclude disruptive pupils (here some changes are underway). Incompatible or barely compatible requirements *invite* compromises and evasions; they undermine both professional judgement and institutional autonomy.

In theory again the new culture of accountability and audit makes professionals and institutions more accountable *for good performance*. This is manifest in the rhetoric of improvement and rising standards, of efficiency gains and best practice, of respect for patients and pupils and employees. But beneath this admirable rhetoric the real focus is on performance indicators chosen for ease of measurement and control rather than because they measure quality of performance accurately. Most people working in the public service have a reasonable sense not only of the specific clinical, educational, policing or other goals for which they work, but also of central ethical standards that they must meet. They know that these complex sets of goals may have to be relegated if they are required to run in a race to improve performance indicators. Even those who devise the indicators know that they are *at very best* surrogates for the real objectives. Nobody after all seriously thinks that numbers of exam passes are the only evidence of good teaching, or that crime clear-up rates are the only evidence of good policing. Some exams are easier, others are harder; some crimes are easier to clear up, others are harder. However, the performance indicators have a deep effect on professional and institutional behaviour. If a certain 'A'-level board offers easier examinations in a subject, schools have reason to choose that syllabus *even if it is educationally inferior.* If waiting lists can be reduced faster by concentrating on certain medical procedures, hospitals have reason so to do, even if medical priorities differ. *Perverse incentives are real incentives.* I think we all know that from our daily lives. Much of the mistrust and criticism now directed at professionals and public institutions complains about their diligence in responding to incentives *to which they have been required to respond* rather than pursuing the intrinsic requirements for being good nurses and teachers, good doctors and police officers, good lecturers and social workers. But what else are they to do under present regimes of accountability?

In the end, the new culture of accountability provides incentives for arbitrary and unprofessional choices. Lecturers may publish prematurely because their department's research rating and its funding require it. Schools may promote certain subjects in which it is easier to get 'As' in public examinations. Hospital Trusts have to focus on waiting lists even where these are not the most significant measures of medical quality. To add to their grief, the Sisyphean task of pushing institutional performance up the league tables is made harder by constantly redefining and adding targets and introducing initiatives, and of course with no account taken of the costs of competing for initiative funding.

In the New World of accountability, conscientious professionals often find that the public *claim* to mistrust them – *but still demand their services.* Claims

of mistrust are poor reward for meeting requirements that allegedly embody higher standards of
public accountability. In ancient Troy the prophetess
Cassandra told the truth, but she wasn't believed.
Like Cassandra, professionals and institutions doing
trustworthy work today may find that the public say
that they do not trust them – but (unlike Cassandra)
their services are still demanded. The pursuit of ever
more perfect accountability provides citizens and
consumers, patients and parents with more information, more comparisons, more complaints systems;
but it also builds a culture of suspicion, low morale,
and may ultimately lead to professional cynicism,
and then we would have grounds for public mistrust.

4 Real accountability?

Perhaps the present revolution in accountability will
make us all trustworthier. Perhaps we shall be trusted
once again. But I think that this is a vain hope – not
because accountability is undesirable or unnecessary,
but because currently fashionable methods of

accountability damage rather than repair trust. If we want greater accountability without damaging professional performance we need *intelligent accountability*. What might this include?

Let me share my sense of some of the possibilities. Intelligent accountability, I suspect, requires more attention to good governance and fewer fantasies about total control. Good governance is possible only if institutions are allowed some margin for self-governance of a form appropriate to their particular tasks, within a framework of financial and other reporting. Such reporting, I believe, is not improved by being wholly standardised or relentlessly detailed, and since much that has to be accounted for is not easily measured it cannot be boiled down to a set of stock performance indicators. Those who are called to account should give an *account* of what they have done, and of their successes or failures, to others who have sufficient time and experience to assess the evidence and report on it. Real accountability provides substantive and knowledgeable independent judgement of an institution's or professional's work.

Well, have we begun to shift? Are we moving

towards less distorting forms of accountability? I think there are a few, but only a few, encouraging straws in the wind. The Kennedy Report into events at the Bristol Royal Infirmary recommends more supportive forms of inspection for Health Trusts and the abolition of the clinical negligence system. There are murmurs about achieving a lighter touch in auditing teaching in those universities that are demonstrably doing it reasonably well. The Education Bill now before Parliament proposes slight exemptions from monitoring for top-performing schools. But these are only small signs of changing ideas. Serious and effective accountability, I believe, needs to concentrate on good governance, on obligations to tell the truth and on intelligent accountability. I think we need to fantasise much less about Herculean micro-management by means of performance indicators or total transparency. If we want a culture of public service, professionals and public servants must in the end be free to serve the public rather than their paymasters.

4

Trust and transparency

1 Trust and information

Socrates did not want his words to go fatherless into the world, transcribed onto tablets or into books that could circulate without their author, to travel beyond the reach of discussion and questions, revision and authentication. So he talked and chatted and argued with others on the streets of Athens, but he wrote and published nothing. (Plato disregarded his teacher's worry and published Socrates' thoughts and conversations anyhow – to our benefit.) The problems to which Socrates pointed are acute in an age of recirculated 'news', public relations, global gossip and Internet publication. How can we tell which claims and counterclaims, reports and supposed facts are trustworthy when so much information swirls around us? It is hard to distinguish rumour from report, fact from fiction, reliable source from disinformant, truth-teller from deceiver.

A crisis of trust cannot be overcome by a blind rush to place more trust. Our ambition is not to place trust blindly, as small children do, but with good judgement. In judging whether to place our trust in others' words or undertakings, or to refuse that trust, we need information and we need the means to judge that information. To place trust reasonably we need to discover not only *which* claims or undertakings we are invited to trust, but *what* we might reasonably think about them.

Reasonably placed trust requires not only information about the proposals or undertakings that others put forward, but also information about those who put them forward. Gullible people who put their trust eagerly in blind dates, or pyramid selling schemes, or snake oil merchants and other unlikely purveyors of sure-fire magic do so on the basis of patently inadequate evidence about those who make the proposals they accept; they get our pity or derision, but hardly our sympathy. We reserve that sympathy for people who cannot judge those who deceived them. If we are to place trust with assurance we need to know *what* we are asked to believe or accept, and *who* is soliciting our trust. Here, it may seem, we are in plenty of luck.

There has never been more abundant information about the individuals and institutions whose claims we have to judge. Openness and transparency are now possible on a scale of which past ages could barely dream. We are flooded with information about government departments and government policies, about public opinion and public debate, about school, hospital and university league tables. We can read facts and figures that supposedly demonstrate financial and professional accountability, cascades of rebarbative semi-technical detail about products and services on the market, and lavish quantities of information about the companies that produce them. At the click of a mouse those with insatiable appetites for information can find out who runs major institutions, look at the home pages and research records of individual scientists, inspect the grants policies of research councils and major charities, download the annual reports and the least thrilling press releases of countless minor public, professional and charitable organisations, not to mention peruse the agenda and the minutes of increasing numbers of public bodies. It seems that no information about institutions and professions is too boring or too routine to remain unpublished. So if making *more* information about *more* public policies, institutions and professionals *more* widely and freely available is the key to building trust, we must be well on the high road towards an ever more trusting society.

This high road is built on new technologies that are ideal for achieving transparency and openness. It has become cheap and easy to spread information, indeed extraordinarily hard to prevent its spread. Secrecy was technically feasible in the days of words on paper. But it is undermined by easy, instantaneous, multiple replication – and endless possibilities for subtle or less-than-subtle revision. We may still speak quaintly of 'leaks' of sensitive information, as if information could be sealed in watertight compartments and archives. But in fact we live amid electronic networks through which information travels with ease, at almost no cost in time, skill or money. Special regimes for data protection and for penalising breaches of commercial or other specific sorts of confidentiality are needed to retain even limited areas of secrecy. Openness or transparency is now all too easy: if it can produce or restore trust, trust should surely be within our grasp.

But during the decades in which new information technologies have come into widespread use, there has been huge optimism about the beneficial effects of wider and more inclusive transparency and openness. 'Open government' has become a watchword. Those holding public office in the UK are required to conform to the seven 'Nolan' principles. These principles demand *selflessness, integrity, objectivity, account-ability, openness, honesty* and *leadership.* Their common core (leadership, perhaps, apart) is a demand for trustworthiness in public life. Newspapers and activists invoke a supposed public 'right to know'. Freedom of information has become an admired ideal, and freedom of the press is still going strong. We are all admonished to make sure that transactions with members of the public are always based on informed consent. It seems that openness and transparency are set to replace traditions of secrecy and deference, at least in public life. Only 'personal data' supplied by individuals for specified purposes are to be protected from disclosure, and here again technology supposedly rides to the rescue, providing new standards of encryption and hence new possibilities for data protection. Ideals of transparency and openness are now so little questioned that those who 'leak' or disseminate confidential information (other than personal data) often expect applause rather than condemnation, and assume that they act in the public interest rather than betray it.

Yet this high enthusiasm for ever more complete openness and transparency has done little to build or restore public trust. On the contrary, trust seemingly has receded as transparency has advanced. Perhaps on reflection we should not be wholly surprised. It is quite clear that the very technologies that spread information so easily and efficiently are every bit as good at spreading misinformation and disinformation. Some sorts of openness and transparency may be bad for trust.

In fact, our clearest images of trust do not link it to openness or transparency at all. Family life is often based on high and reciprocal trust, but close relatives do not always burden one another with full disclosure of their financial or professional dealings, let alone with comprehensive information about their love lives or health problems; and they certainly do not disclose family information promiscuously to all the world. Similarly, in trusting doctor–patient relationships (that's the sort we supposedly no longer enjoy) medically relevant information was disclosed under conditions of confidence. Mutual respect *precludes* rather than *requires* across-the-board openness between doctor and patient, and disclosure of confidential information beyond the relationship is wholly unacceptable. I may trust my friends, colleagues and neighbours wholeheartedly, without any wish, or need, to know everything about their private lives – or to have them know everything about mine.

Perhaps it is not then surprising that public distrust has grown in the very years in which openness and transparency have been so avidly pursued.

Transparency certainly destroys secrecy: but it may not limit the deception and deliberate misinformation that undermine relations of trust. If we want to restore trust we need to reduce *deception and lies* rather than *secrecy*. Some sorts of secrecy indeed support deception, others do not. Transparency and openness may not be the unconditional goods that they are fashionably supposed to be. By the same token, secrecy and lack of transparency may not be the enemies of trust.

2 Deception and misinformation

I think that deception is the real enemy of trust. Deception is not just a matter of getting things wrong. It can be pretty irritating to be misled by somebody's honest mistake, but it is not nearly as bad as being their dupe. The passer-by who in all honesty provides a stranger with inaccurate directions for reaching a destination or the club secretary who in all honesty sends out notices for a meeting giving the wrong date are not deceivers. Nor, irritating as they may be, are those who in all honesty undertake to perform tasks that are beyond their competence. Deceivers by contrast mislead intentionally, and it is because their falsehood is deliberate, and because it implies a deliberate intention to undermine, damage or distort others' plans and their capacities to act, that it damages trust and future relationships.

Deception is not a minor or a marginal moral failure. Deceivers do not treat others as moral equals; they exempt themselves from obligations that they rely on others to live up to. Deception lies at the heart of many serious crimes, including fraud and embezzlement, impersonation and obtaining goods by false pretences, forgery and counterfeiting, perjury and spying, smuggling and false accounting, slander and libel. Deception is also part of nearly all theft and most crimes of violence and coercion: burglars enter houses surreptitiously; spies and terrorists establish bogus credentials, live under assumed names, conduct spurious businesses and form deceptive friendships; murderers often lull their victims into false security and lure them to their deaths. Deceptions may amount to treachery or betrayal.

Soviet historians lyingly misrepresented the massacre of Polish officers at Katyn as a German rather than a Soviet war crime; Judas Iscariot falsely played the part of the faithful disciple; Macbeth falsely acted the part of Duncan's faithful vassal. Wolves who wear sheep's (or grandmothers') clothing are not just making mistakes. Nor are card cheats and plagiarists, those who promote false history or scientific fraud, those who write false references for friends (or for colleagues whom they want to shed) or those who corruptly swing contracts, jobs or other favours in the direction of their cronies. Nor are those who hide their conflicts of interest, who promise commitments they have no intention of honouring, or who two-time their partners.

If we want to increase trust we need to avoid *deception* rather than *secrecy*. Although some ways of increasing transparency may indirectly reduce deception, many do not. Unless there has been prior deception, transparency does nothing to reduce deception; and even if there has been deception, openness is not a sure-fire remedy. Increasing transparency can produce a flood of unsorted information and misinformation that provides little but confusion unless it can be sorted and assessed. It may add to uncertainty rather than to trust. And unless the individuals and institutions who sort, process and assess information are themselves already trusted, there is little reason to think that transparency and openness are going to increase trust. Transparency can encourage people to be less honest, so increasing deception and reducing reasons for trust: those who know that *everything* they say or write is to be made public may massage the truth. Public reports may underplay sensitive information; head teachers and employers may write blandly uninformative reports and references; evasive and uninformative statements may substitute for truth-telling. Demands for universal transparency are likely to encourage the evasions, hypocrisies and half-truths that we usually refer to as 'political correctness', but which might more forthrightly be called either 'self-censorship' or 'deception'.

There are deeper and more systematic reasons for thinking that transparency damages trust. We can only judge whether there is deception, hence reason not to place trust, when we can tell whether we have been fed deliberate falsehoods. But how can we do this when we cannot even tell *who* has asserted, compiled or endorsed the supposed information? In a world in which information and misinformation are 'generated', in which good drafting is a vanishing art, in which so-called information 'products' can be transmitted, reformatted and adjusted, embroidered and elaborated, shaped and spun, repeated and respun, it can be quite hard to assess truth or false-hood.

Paradoxically then, in the new information order, those who choose to make up information or to pass it on without checking its accuracy have rather an easy time. Positions are often maintained in the face of widely available and well-authenticated contrary evidence. Supposed sources proliferate, leaving many of us unsure where and whether there is adequate evidence for or against contested claims. In spite of ample sources we may be left uncertain about the supposed evidence that certain drugs are risky, or that fluoride in the water harms, or that standards for environmental pollutants in water or air have been set too high (or too low or at the right level), that professional training of doctors or teachers is adequate or inadequate, that waste disposal by incineration or by landfill is safer. Proponents of views on these and countless other points may not heed available evidence and can mount loud and assertive campaigns for or against one or another position *whether the available evidence goes for or against their views*. As the quantity of (mis)information available rises, as the number of bodies with self-conferred credentials and missions and active publicity machines increases, as the difficulty of knowing whether a well-publicised claim is a credible claim increases, it is simply harder to place trust reasonably. Milton asked rhetorically 'Who ever knew truth put to the worse in a free and open encounter?' Today the very prospect of a 'free and open encounter' is drowning in the supposedly transparent world of the new information order.

3 Information and informed consent

Global transparency and complete openness are not the best ways to build or restore trust. We place and refuse trust not because we have torrents of information (more is not always better), but because we can trace *specific* bits of information and *specific* undertakings to *particular* sources on whose veracity and reliability we can run some checks. *Well-placed trust grows out of active inquiry rather than blind acceptance.* In traditional relations of trust, active inquiry was usually extended over time by talking and asking questions, by listening and seeing how well claims to know and undertakings to act held up. That was the world in which Socrates placed his trust – and his reservations about publishing. Where we can check the information we receive, and when we can go back to those who put it into circulation, we may gain confidence about placing or refusing trust.

But where we can do nothing to check or investigate sources of information and their credentials we often, and reasonably, withhold trust and suspend both belief and disbelief in favour of cynicism and half-belief. We may end up *claiming* not to trust, and yet *for practical purposes* place trust in the very sources we claim not to trust. Where possibilities for checking and questioning supposed information are fragmented, trust too may fragment. Even if we do not end up with a crisis of trust we end up with a culture of suspicion.

So if we want a society in which placing trust is feasible we need to look for ways in which we can actively check one another's claims. Active checking has to be more than a matter of checking that many sources of information concur: reading extra copies of a newspaper or extra newspapers lends no extra credibility. Nor can active checking reduce to citing sources such as well-frequented or favourite websites and channels: arguments from authority, to use the old term, however deliciously congruent with favourite beliefs, establish nothing. In an information order in which 'sources' borrow promiscuously from one another, in which statistics are cited and regurgitated because they look striking or convenient for those pursuing some agenda, in which rumour can readily be reprocessed as news, active checking of information is pretty hard for many of us. Unqualified trust is then understandably rather scarce.

Ought we then to conclude that unqualified trust belongs only in face-to-face relationships, where information is provided directly by people we know, whom we can question and monitor? Certainly direct relationships between individuals – intimate or not – can be good for establishing trust, but they are not enough. We need to place or refuse trust far more widely.

We can place trust beyond face-to-face relationships when we can check the information and undertakings others offer. This is after all the function of informed consent requirements, where consent is given or refused in the light of information that should be checkable. Informed consent procedures have a place all the way from choosing socks to choosing university courses, from getting an inoculation to getting married, from choosing a video to choosing a career. Of course, even if all informed consent were given in the light of good and trustworthy information, those who consent can get things wrong. They may choose flimsy socks and boring videos, they may marry philanderers and embark on university courses with which they cannot cope. There are no guarantees. But informed consent can provide a basis for trust *provided* that those who are to consent are not offered a flood of uncheckable information, but rather information whose accuracy they can check and assess for themselves. This is demanding.

Capacities for testing others' credibility and reliability often fail and falter. Sometimes they falter because the information provided is too arcane and obscure. But sometimes they fail because those asked to consent cannot check and test the information they are offered, so can't work out whether they are being deceived, or whether they can reasonably place their trust. So Socrates' misgivings are not obsolete today. It is very easy to imagine that in a world in which information travels like quicksilver, trust can do the same. It cannot. Placing trust is, I suggest, as demanding today as it was in Athens.

5

Licence to deceive?

1 Testing and trusting

We all know the story of the hero who goes courting a Princess. Her father sends him on demanding quests in distant lands. On the face of it this is not the ideal preparation for marriage, or for ruling the kingdom. But the point of the quest, as we all know, is that the King needs to judge the hero's commitment and steadfastness. If the hero persists in his quest the King will have reason to trust him; if Princess and hero remain steadfast through long years of questing, each will have reason to trust the other's love and loyalty, and they will live happily ever after. Quests are *tests of trustworthiness.*

Everyday tests of trustworthiness are simpler. A brief exchange of words, a few questions, a short meeting and we begin to place some trust, which we revise, extend or reduce as we observe and check performance. But how are we to test strangers and institutions? How can we judge claims and undertakings when we can't talk with others, or observe them, let alone send them on lengthy quests? How can we tell that they are not deceiving us?

Perhaps we are in luck. We live in an age of communication technologies. It should be easier than it used to be to check out strangers and institutions, to test credentials, to authenticate sources and to place trust well. But unfortunately many of the new ways of communicating don't offer adequate, let alone easy, ways of doing so. The new information technologies are ideal for spreading reliable information, but they dislocate our ordinary ways of judging one another's claims and deciding where to place our trust.

When Kings of old tested their daughters' suitors, most communication was face-to-face and two-way; in the information age it is often between strangers and one-way. Socrates worried about the written word, because it travelled beyond the possibility of question and revision, and so beyond trust. We may reasonably worry not only about the written word, but also about broadcast speech, film and television. These technologies are designed for one-way communication with minimal interaction. Those who control and use them may or may not be trustworthy. How are we to check what they tell us?

2 Informed consent and trust

Informed consent is one hallmark of trust between strangers. When I understand a pension plan, a mortgage or complex medical procedures, and am free to choose or refuse, I express trust by giving informed consent. We give informed consent in face-to-face transactions too, but we barely notice it. We buy apples in the market, exchange addresses with acquaintances and sit down for a haircut. It sounds pompous to speak of these daily transactions as based on *informed consent*; yet in each we assume that the other party is neither deceiving nor coercing. We withdraw trust very fast if we are sold rotten apples, deliberately given a false address or forcibly subjected to a Mohican haircut. Everyday trust is utterly undermined by coercion or deception.

Informed consent is supposed to guarantee individual *autonomy* or *independence.* This popular thought is pretty obscure, because so many views of autonomy are in play. Some people identify individual autonomy with *spontaneous choosing.* A New York student of mine once stripped and streaked across Broadway with a group of male contemporaries, and so convinced herself that she was *autonomous.* She had at least shown that she could act in defiance of convention, and probably of her parents, but hardly of her male contemporaries. Her eccentric choice was at least harmless, but in other cases *spontaneous choosing* can be harmful or disastrous. Other people identify individual autonomy not with *spontaneous* but with *deliberate choosing.* But deliberate choosing doesn't guarantee much either. The real importance of informed consent, I believe, has little to do with *how* we choose. Informed consent is just as important when we make conventional and timid choices, or thoughtless and unreflective choices, as it is when we choose deliberately and independently. Informed consent matters simply because it shows that a transaction is not based on deception or coercion.

Informed consent is always important, but it isn't the basis of trust. On the contrary, it *presupposes* and *expresses* trust, which we must already place to assess the information we're given. Should I have a proposed operation? Should I buy this car or that computer? Is this Internet bargain genuine? In each case I need to assess what is offered, but may be unable to judge the information for myself. Others' expert judgement may fill the gap: I may rely on the surgeon who explains the operation, or on a colleague who knows about cars or computers or Internet shopping. But in relying on others I already place trust in my adviser: as Francis Bacon noted, 'the greatest trust between man and man is the trust of giving counsel.'[1] When we draw on friendly – or on expert – help we ultimately have to *judge for ourselves where to place our trust*. To do this we need to find trustworthy information. This can be dauntingly hard in a world of one-way communication.

1 Francis Bacon, Essays xx, *Of Counsel* (Oxford: Clarendon Press, 2000).

3 Trust and the media

In an age of mass communication, information is abundant, but often mixed with misinformation and disinformation. It can be hard to check and test what we read and hear. There are easy cases: we can check weather forecasts for their accuracy by waiting for tomorrow; we can rumble supermarkets that don't sell goods at advertised prices. But there are hard cases: how can parents judge whether to have a child vaccinated or to refuse a vaccination? How can we tell whether a product or a service will live up to its billing? Yet for daily and practical purposes we need to place our trust in some strangers and some institutions, and to refuse it to others. How can we do this well?

We know what we need. We need ways of telling trustworthy from untrustworthy informants. And we have tried to make this possible by promoting a revolution in accountability and requirements for transparency in public life. I have argued in previous chapters that we need more intelligent forms of accountability, and to focus less on grandiose ideals of transparency and rather more on limiting deception. Do we really gain from heavy-handed accountability that combines managerial targets with requirements for detailed compliance with bureaucratic process? I am unconvinced. I think we may undermine professional performance and standards by excessive regulation, and that we may condone deception in our zeal for total transparency.

And meanwhile some powerful institutions and professions have escaped the revolutions in accountability and transparency. Most evidently, the media, in particular the print media – while deeply preoccupied with others' untrustworthiness – have escaped demands for accountability (apart from the financial disciplines set by company law and accounting practices). This is less true of the terrestrial broadcasting media, which are subject to the Broadcasting Act 1996 and the Broadcasting Standards Commission. The BBC also has its *Charter, Agreement* and *Producers' Guidelines,*[2] which include commitments to *impartiality, accuracy, fairness, giving a full view, editorial*

2 British Broadcasting Corporation, *Producers' Guidelines: The BBC's Values and Standards* (London: BBC, 2000).

independence, respect for privacy, standards of taste and *decency.* (I make no comment on compliance.)

Newspaper editors and journalists are not held accountable in these ways. Outstanding reporting and writing mingle with editing and reporting that smears, sneers and jeers, names, shames and blames. Some reporting 'covers' (should I say 'uncovers'?) dementing amounts of trivia, some misrepresents and denigrates, some teeters on the brink of defamation. In this curious world, commitments to trustworthy reporting are erratic: there is no shame in writing on matters beyond a reporter's competence, in coining misleading headlines, in omitting matters of public interest or importance, or in recirculating others' speculations as 'news'. Above all there is no requirement to make evidence accessible to the readers.

For all of us who have to place trust with care in a complex world, reporting that we cannot assess is a disaster. If we can't trust what the press report, how can we tell whether to trust those on whom they report? An erratically reliable or unassessable press may not matter for privileged people with other sources of information, who can tell which stories are near the mark and which confused, vicious or simply false; *but for most citizens it matters.* How can we tell whether newspapers, websites and publications that claim to be 'independent' are promoting some agenda? How can we tell whether and when we are on the receiving end of hype and spin, of misinformation and disinformation? There is a lot of more or less accurate reporting, but this is small comfort if readers can't tell which are the reliable bits. What we need is reporting that we can assess and check – what we get often can't be assessed or checked by non-experts. If the media mislead, or if readers cannot assess their reporting, the wells of public discourse are poisoned. The new information technologies may be anti-authoritarian, but curiously they are often used in ways that are anti-democratic. They undermine our capacities to judge others' claims and to place our trust.

4 Press freedom
in the twenty-first century

So if we want to address the supposed 'crisis of trust'
it will not be enough to discipline government, business or the professions – or all of them. We also will
need to develop a more robust public culture, in
which publishing misinformation and disinformation, and writing in ways that others cannot hope to
check, are limited and penalised. Yet can we do so and
keep a free press?

We may use twenty-first-century communication
technologies, but we cherish nineteenth-century
views of freedom of the press, paradigmatically those
of John Stuart Mill. When Mill wrote, the press in
many countries was censored. The wonderful images
of a free press speaking truth to power and of inves-
tigative journalists as tribunes of the people belong to
those more dangerous and heroic times. In democra-
cies the image is obsolescent: journalists face little
danger (except on overseas assignments) and the
press do not risk being closed down. On the contrary,

the press has acquired unaccountable power that others cannot match.

Rather to my surprise and comfort, the classic arguments for press freedom do not endorse, let alone require, a press with unaccountable power. *A free press can be and should be an accountable press.*

Accountability does not mean censorship: it precludes censorship. Nobody should dictate what may be published, beyond narrowly drawn requirements to protect public safety, decency and personal privacy. But freedom of the press also does not require a licence to deceive. Like Mill we want the press to be free to seek truth and to challenge accepted views. But writing that seeks truth, or (more modestly) tries not to mislead, needs internal disciplines and standards to make it assessable and criticisable by its readers. There is no case for a licence to spread confusion or obscure the truth, to overwhelm the public with 'information overload', or an even more dispiriting 'misinformation overload', let alone to peddle and rehearse disinformation.

Like Mill we may be passionate about individual

freedom of expression, and so about the freedom of the press to represent individuals' opinions and views. But freedom of expression is for individuals, not for institutions. We have good reasons for allowing individuals to express opinions even if they are invented, false, silly, irrelevant or plain crazy, but not for allowing powerful institutions to do so. Yet we are perilously close to a world in which media conglomerates act as if they too had unrestricted rights of free expression, and therefore a licence to subject positions for which they don't care to caricature and derision, misrepresentation or silence. If they had those unconditional rights they would have rights to undermine individuals' abilities to judge for themselves and to place their trust well, indeed rights to undermine democracy.

Like Mill we may support freedom of discussion, think that it is fundamental to democracy, and so support the freedom of the press to foster what in the USA is charmingly called *wide-open, robust debate.* But for that very reason we cannot support freedom for media conglomerates to orchestrate public 'discussion' in which some or many voices are unrepresented or caricatured, in which misinformation may be peddled uncorrected and in which reputations may be selectively shredded or magnified.

A free press is not an unconditional good. Press freedom is good because and insofar as it helps the public to explore and test opinions and to judge for themselves *whom* and *what* to believe and trust. If powerful institutions are allowed to publish, circulate and promote material without indicating what is known and what is rumour, what is derived from a reputable source and what is invented, what is standard analysis and what is speculation, which sources may be knowledgeable and which are probably not, they damage our public culture and all our lives. Good public debate must not only be *accessible to* but also *assessable by* its audiences. The press are skilled at making material accessible, but erratic about making it assessable. This may be why opinion polls and social surveys now show that the public in the UK claim that they trust newspaper journalists less than any other profession, and incidentally substantially less than they trust radio and television journalists.

5 Assessable communication and Kantian autonomy

The received wisdom on press freedom assumes that freedoms and rights can be free-standing. In fact there are no rights without counterpart obligations. Respecting obligations is as vital for communication as for other activities. At the very least we have obligations to communicate in ways that do not destroy or undermine others' prospects of communicating. Yet deceivers do just this. They communicate in ways that others cannot share and follow, test and check, and thereby damage others' communication and action. They undermine the very trust on which communication itself depends: they free-ride on others' trust and truthfulness.

Obligations not to deceive are more closely connected to Kant's rather than Mill's conception of autonomy. Kantian autonomy is a matter of acting on principles that can be principles for all, of ensuring that we do not treat others as lesser mortals – indeed victims – whom we may disable from sharing our principles. If we deceive we make others our victims, and undermine or distort their possibilities for acting and communicating. We arrogantly base our own communication and action on principles that destroy trust, and so limit others' possibilities for action. Ways of communicating can be unacceptable for many reasons: threats may intimidate and coerce; slander may injure. But the most common wrong done in communicating is deception, which undermines and damages others' capacities to judge and communicate, to act and to place trust with good judgement. Obligations to reject deception are obligations for everyone: for individuals and for government and for institutions – including the media and journalists.

At present the public have few reliable ways of detecting whether reporting is deceptive or not. We could improve matters without any trace of censorship, and without imposing regulatory burdens of the excessive and centralising sorts that are failing us elsewhere. A lot could be altered by procedural changes, such as requirements for owners, editors and journalists to declare financial and other interests (and conflicts of interest), and to distinguish comment from reporting, or by penalties for recirculating rumours others publish without providing evidence. Chequebook journalism could be reduced by requirements to disclose within any 'story' *who* paid *whom* how much for any 'contribution'. I am still looking for ways to ensure that journalists do not publish 'stories' for which there is no source at all, while pretending that there is a source to be protected.

Only if we build a public culture – and above all a media culture – in which we can rely on others not to deceive us will we be able to judge whom and what we can reasonably trust. If we remain cavalier about press standards, a culture of suspicion will persist. We will still place our trust for practical purposes, but we will do so suspiciously and unhappily. Our present culture of suspicion cannot be dispelled by making everyone except the media trustworthier. To restore trust we need not only trustworthy persons and institutions, but also *assessable reasons for trusting and for mistrusting.* These cannot be found by rehearsing suspicions, or by recirculating them again and again, without providing evidence.

We *say* that we want to end the supposed crisis of public trust, and we've tried to do so in part by making many professions and institutions trustworthier. In these chapters I have queried both diagnosis and remedy. We may constantly express suspicion, but it is not at all clear that we have stopped placing our trust in others – indeed that may be impossible. We may constantly seek to make others trustworthy, but some of the regimes of accountability and transparency developed across the last fifteen years may damage rather than reinforce trustworthiness. The intrusive methods we have taken to stem a supposed crisis of trust may even, if things go badly, fuel a crisis of trustworthiness, and so lead to a genuine crisis of trust.

If we want to avoid this unfortunate spiral we need to think less about accountability through micromanagement and central control, and more about good governance; less about transparency and more about limiting deception. If we are to restore trust we shall have to start communicating in ways that are open to assessment, and to do this we need to rethink the proper limits of press freedom. The press has no licence to deceive; and we have no reasons to think that a free press needs such licence.